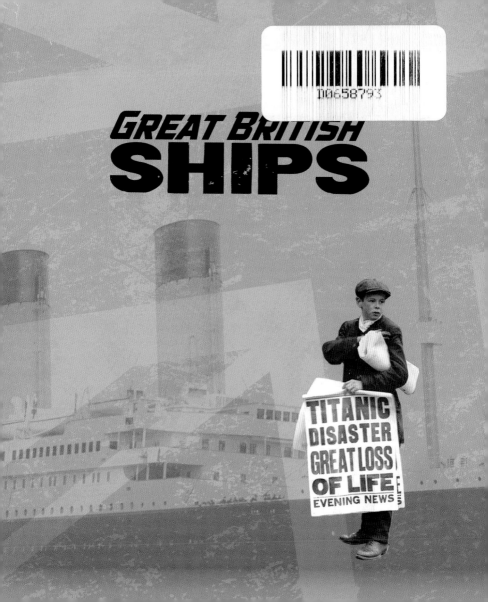

GREAT BRITISH
SHIPS

TITANIC
DISASTER
GREAT LOSS
OF LIFE
EVENING NEWS

GREAT BRITISH SHIPS
A PICTORIAL HISTORY

MIRCO DE CET

AURA

This edition published in 2019
by Baker & Taylor (UK) Ltd,
Bicester, Oxfordshire, OX26 4ST

Copyright © Arcturus Holdings Limited
26/27 Bickels Yard, 151–153 Bermondsey Street
London SE1 3HA

ISBN: 978-1-78888-927-8
AD007193UK

Printed in China

Contents

Introduction

'Rule, Britannia! Britannia rules the waves'.

'Rule, Britannia!' is a patriotic song written by exiled Scottish poet James Thomson and set to music by Thomas Arne in 1740. It was originally conceived to help unite the English, Welsh, Scots and Irish as one nation under a new British identity. It has come to be closely associated with the Royal Navy as well as a certain strain of jingoistic pride that arrived with empire and Britain's heyday as the leading world power in the 19th and early 20th centuries.

It can be hard to understand how such a tiny island tucked away in the North Atlantic could have made such an impact on the world. It was thanks largely

The bronze statue of Britannia at Plymouth Hoe, from where the Spanish Armada was first spotted.

A decorative plate made in Liverpool, 1793–94, that lauds the seafaring tradition.

to Britain's seafaring traditions that people were able to travel huge distances across oceans, transporting and distributing their ideas, imposing their beliefs upon others and extracting wealth from distant lands.

As an island race, the British had to invent seaworthy vessels to trade with people across the waters. The first boats capable of travelling to other countries are thought to have been coracles or even basket boats. These small vessels were propelled either by oars or a small sail (sometimes a combination of both). Later, Aethelred II raised a formidable fleet through a national levy of one ship for every 310 hides of land. During the time of Danish rule in England in the 11th century, the government maintained a standing fleet through taxation; and long before that, the Anglo-Saxons had introduced a 'ship-mustering system' called the *scipfryd*.

Through his Crusades, King Richard I learned about ship design from the Mediterranean boat-builders. He saw how the forecastle and aftercastle added vital cabin space; this style would become a feature of the English ocean-going trade ship. By the Middle Ages, sail had taken over from oars, although muscle power still helped to steer the ship. Soon afterwards, a rudder was attached, initially to the side of the ship, but later at the rear in the position used today. The compass was introduced, but the subtleties of using such a sophisticated instrument took time to understand. By the 15th century, fully rigged ships were introduced in the wake of successful explorers such as Vasco da Gama, Columbus and Cabot. As ships travelled further afield and their cargoes grew larger, speed became crucial. This was achieved with the addition of more sails via multiple masts. During peacetime, ships happily traded between nations, although some carried guns for protection. As the size and number of guns increased, ships no longer had as much room for cargo, and in times of conflict, they began to travel in convoy, with pure warships protecting the merchant craft from enemies such as pirates and privateers.

By defeating the navies of its greatest enemies – France, Spain and to a lesser extent the Netherlands – Britain became great. Many legends were made at sea. As a privateer naval officer, Sir Francis Drake carried out the second circumnavigation of the world and dabbled in the slave trade during the Elizabethan era. Captain James Cook was an explorer, navigator and cartographer. He drew up detailed maps of Newfoundland before making three voyages to the Pacific Ocean, where he was the first European to visit the eastern coastline of Australia and the Hawaiian Islands. The legendary Vice Admiral Horatio Nelson, noted for his inspirational leadership, grasp of strategy, and unconventional tactics, brought

HMS Vengeance, *a modern nuclear sub – the name alone sends shivers up the spine.*

about a number of famous British naval victories; the best known was Trafalgar, where he also forfeited his life.

Great British Ships documents Britain's amazing naval history and the ships that made the nation prosper. It features renowned ships such as the *Cutty Sark* and the *Golden Hind*, but includes many lesser known vessels from different eras.

Today, the Royal Navy has 74 commissioned ships. Almost all the ships and submarines currently in commission with the Royal Navy were built in the United Kingdom. Carrying on the great naval tradition, a new aircraft carrier, HMS *Queen Elizabeth*, left Rosyth dockyard in June 2017 to commence sea trials. A second carrier is being built, HMS *Prince of Wales*, and it should be ready for front-line duties around the globe from 2023.

While Britain may no longer rule the waves, she still has much influence at sea and has unquestionably paved the way for, and advanced the building of, some of the world's most important and sophisticated ships.

An Island Race

Pre-history to 1837

When the ice sheets of the last glaciation period retreated, the British Isles as we know them first appeared; this happened some 13,000 years ago. Since it is an island, Britain's history has always been tied to its waters. Migration, military adventure and solid commerce over the centuries were to see England, in particular, become a major trading and naval power via the building and use of ships and boats.

Through archaeological digs and finds, considerable information has come to light concerning the earliest ships and boats. Many of the remains have been found on land rather than at sea, this being due to the change in land-mass and shifting weather systems over the years.

When the British Isles were separated from mainland Europe, some form of vessel would have been necessary to make contact across the English Channel and the southern reaches of the North Sea. It is thought that multiple hide boats, similar to coracles, and even basket boats, would have been able to carry out sea voyages at that time.

During the Neolithic period, contact between Britain, Ireland and mainland Europe would probably have developed across the 'Western Seaways', which covered an area of sea roughly from the Channel Islands in the south, through the Scilly Isles, the Isle of Man, and the Hebrides up as far as the Orkneys. Although there is some doubt as to how far they could safely navigate offshore, the remains of Neolithic dugout canoes have been found in several parts of England.

Men and women fish from a dugout canoe, while others in the background just stand in the river and spear fish.

A scene showing Neolithic people with their coracles.

Early men make dugouts by burning and scraping trees with seashells.

Left and below: *In 1981, the remains of a logboat were found by the River Meese at Chetwynd Park, Shropshire. The boat was incomplete and damaged by extraction, but the wood was well preserved. It had been constructed from half an oak log. The overall shape of the craft was flat bottomed with a sharply rising bow.*

This odd piece of wood was once a logboat, which was made some 2,300 years ago. It is estimated that this tree would have been about 1.7 metres wide (5.5 ft) and would already have been 150 to 200 years old before being cut down.

The three Ferriby boats were found at the Humber estuary. A small-scale model shows what they would have looked like (below) and, on the left, is the memorial where they were discovered.

The next stage in vessel building was plank construction, where timber was cut and shaped by an axe, then fastened together – mostly stitched – to create a watertight hull. Early examples of stitched boats were found at Ferriby in the East Riding of Yorkshire. These were Middle Bronze Age vessels, some of the earliest known examples worldwide.

Hollowed out from a single massive oak tree, this boat was preserved in the mud of the River Witham for nearly 2,500 years. It was deliberately sunk to the bottom of the river as a religious offering.

Archaeological evidence points to the fact that cross-Channel trade took place well before the Roman conquest of AD 43. This seems to confirm that cargo was being transported by ocean-going vessels and that trade routes were established during the Bronze Age. Numerous Iron Age dugouts have been found in both coastal and inland sites across England, which seems to confirm that these types of boats were used extensively.

By the late Iron Age, ships had advanced in design and accounts in *Commentāriī dē Bellō Gallicō* – commentaries on the Gallic Wars – written by none other than Julius

Caesar, document the changes. In these reports, Caesar includes descriptions of fighting on the Atlantic coast in 56 BC. He explains how the ships of the Gauls were rigged differently from those of the Romans and goes on to say that some of the vessels' timbers included beams a foot wide, fastened with iron bolts 'as thick as a man's thumb'.

In 54 BC, Caesar prepared a second fleet of ships to invade Britain, his first effort having failed. Some 600 vessels set sail, the transport vessels having been modified so as to make them lower and broader, which would help with landing in shallow waters. Also included in his fleet was a large number of warships.

They landed in Kent, but the invasion was shortlived and Caesar soon departed for more pressing matters in Gaul.

An engraving showing Roman ships landing in England.

The Vikings

The first known account of the Vikings raiding Anglo-Saxon England came in 789 when three ships from Hordaland – modern-day Norway – landed on the Isle of Portland on the Dorset coast. They were met by the local reeve – an official elected annually by the serfs to supervise landholdings and identify foreign merchants attempting to infiltrate the kingdom – whom they promptly killed. The *Anglo-Saxon Chronicles* also mentions further raids on London during the 9th century. Vikings invaded with their 'longships' and it is thought that these raids may have triggered increased shipbuilding, which many agree could have been the beginning of a home-grown shipbuilding industry. The *Chronicles* also mentions the fact that, in 896, King Alfred had commissioned a new fleet of 60-oared warships, with which to do battle against the invaders.

Hugin is a replica Viking ship that was sailed from Denmark to Kent in 1949. The trip was made to commemorate the 1,500th anniversary of the arrival of legendary Saxon chieftains Hengist and his brother Horsa. They landed at Ebbsfleet and, soon after, Hengist became the first Saxon King of Kent.

Clinkers

The most common type of vessel at the time of the Norman Conquest was the clinker build (where the edges of hull planks overlap each other), and when the Normans invaded in 1066, their ships carried not only large numbers of men but also horses; these vessels benefited from years of development.

During the Middle Ages, England possessed large tracts of land in France and expanding trade networks required bigger and bigger vessels to cope with increased trade and to defend national assets. While the clinker build generally suited smaller vessels such as 'cogs', the keel technique – building up from a main keel – worked better for larger vessels, such as the 20 war galleys ordered by Edward I in 1294. These were built in preparation for the expected invasion of southern England by the French. This never came.

When the Hanseatic League was formed in the city of Lübeck, now northern Germany, in 1158, it had a huge influence on the type of mercantile vessel that developed. The Hanseatic League was a confederation of merchant guilds and trading towns in north-western and central Europe. Starting out from a handful of north German towns in the late 1100s, gradually the league came to dominate Baltic maritime trade along the coasts of northern Europe that lasted three centuries.

Illustrated documents show that from about 1350 the clear divisions between the keel, hulk and cog types of ship were breaking down. There was an increasing variety of different vessels, among them the carrack, a ship that endured from the 14th to the 17th century and became the forerunner of the now familiar three-masted ships which lasted until the mid-19th century.

Opposite top: *The* Roland von Bremen, *a cog docked at Bremen, 2006.* (Opposite bottom) *The* Ubena von Bremen – *another replica Bremen cog – seen at Kiel Week in 2007, a yearly regatta event.*

During the medieval period, shipbuilding showed marked differences between the north and south of Europe. In the north, the clinker build was popular, but in the south ships had planking; planks were laid out flush and fastened end-to-end in the technique called carvel building.

Documents show that at least one carvel vessel existed in England in the 1460s and another example was found during an excavation at Roff's Wharf, Woolwich. This vessel – believed to be the *Sovereign*, Henry VII's royal ship – was built in 1488.

This is the Henry Grace à Dieu *– meaning 'Henry, thanks be to God' – and nicknamed Great Harry. She was an English carrack and made up part of the king's fleet in the 16th century. The* Grace à Dieu *was Henry VIII's flagship and carried him to the conference with Francis I of France on the Field of the Cloth of Gold, 1520.*

This wall painting of a ship takes pride of place in the north aisle of St Dunstan's Church on Romney Marsh. So good is this painting that it can be dated back to a type of 'great ship' from the period 1480–1520, of perhaps 800 tons, with four masts, a forecastle, half-deck and quarter-deck. There is speculation, although no real evidence, that this could have been the Regent, *part of the royal fleet and a vessel which was destroyed at the Battle of St Matthieu, 1512.*

The *Mary Rose*

The incredible recovery of Henry VIII's flagship, the *Mary Rose*, from the Solent in 1982 was a high point in English maritime archaeology. The ship, begun in 1510, was a purpose-built carrack and had upper-deck gun ports; further heavier guns were added to the main deck, just above the waterline, from around 1536. The *Mary Rose* was lost in 1545 after facing the French during the Battle of the Solent. It is thought that she may have turned sharply, leaned heavily to one side and, with the gun ports still open, taken on water and sunk. Most of the crew went down with the ship.

A photograph from the Mary Rose Museum in Portsmouth, showing the side of the ship that was buried in the mud and silt, which helped to preserve this part of the ship.

Above is the only 16th-century illustration that shows the Mary Rose *for certain. All the green and white streamers point to the ship being in the service of the king.*

The Cowdray engraving showing the Battle of the Solent, 1545. The main and foremasts of the recently sunken Mary Rose *are in the middle of the image; bodies, debris and rigging float in the water and desperate men are clinging to the fighting tops.*

This gun is known as a long-range demi-culverin and was found at the front of the aftercastle – the widest part of a ship – of the Mary Rose. *While this type of gun could fire long distances, it was not ideal for the types of military confrontations of the time, generally hand-to-hand battle. Inscribed on the barrel is: 'Henry the Eighth, by the grace of God, King of England and France, Defender of the Faith, Lord of Ireland and on Earth the Supreme Head of the English church.'*

Main image: *A view of St Mawes Castle, with Pendennis on the opposite side of the estuary in the distance.*

Inset: *Cannons were positioned pointing out to sea, ready to fire at any advancing enemy from across the water.*

The threat from across the water

The threat of invasion offered by the great Catholic powers of France and the Holy Roman Empire from across the water was ever present, probably ensuring the expansion and development of the royal fleet, especially after Henry broke his religious ties with Rome in the mid-1530s. Between 1539 and 1547, Henry ordered the building of 30 coastal 'Artillery Forts' as bulwarks against these hostile enemy powers.

This page:
Deal Castle, Kent.

Opposite: *Walmer Castle, Kent. Again, its guns point out to sea.*

Many experts would agree that this was the start of the Royal Navy. It was certainly the single greatest royal plan for naval expansion seen to date, and with it came the creation of royal dockyards at Deptford, Woolwich, Chatham and Portsmouth.

Further coastal fortifications were added during the reign of Elizabeth I, along with 61 new and rebuilt ships. The enemy now were the Spanish and, in 1558, England lost Calais, their last stronghold on the Continent.

Although it was seen as provocative and certainly illegal, between 1560 and 1570 the English were keen to take advantage of the lucrative Spanish trade with the Americas through a kind of legalized piracy. Much of this new activity was carried out by 'English Privateers', that is, vessels that were authorized by a letter of marque – a government licence that authorized a privateer or corsair to attack and capture enemy vessels.

In late May of 1588, the Spanish amassed a fleet of 130 ships (the Spanish Armada) under the command of the Duke of Medina Sidonia. This set sail from Coruña in north-west Spain with the purpose of escorting an army from Flanders which would then invade England.

The plan was to overthrow Queen Elizabeth I along with Protestantism in England in the hope that this would also put an end to English interference in the Spanish Netherlands, and to the damage being caused to Spanish interests by English and Dutch privateers.

English ships and the Spanish Armada, August 1588.

A portrait made to commemorate the defeat of the Spanish Armada. Elizabeth's international power is reflected by the hand resting on the globe.

The Armada cried off from attacking the English fleet at Plymouth, then failed to establish temporary anchorage in the Solent after a Spanish ship was captured by Sir Francis Drake in the English Channel.

Finally, they dropped anchor off Calais and, while awaiting communications from the Duke of Parma's army, the Armada was scattered by an English fireship attack (ships literally set on fire and sent towards the enemy to cause panic). In the ensuing Battle of Gravelines, the Spanish fleet was damaged and forced to abandon its planned rendezvous with Parma's army, which was blockaded in harbour by Dutch flyboats (large flat-bottomed armed boats). The Armada managed to regroup and withdrew north, with the English fleet chasing it up the east coast of England.

Returning to Spain, it encountered severe storms in the North Atlantic and a large number of vessels were wrecked on the coasts of Scotland and Ireland. Of the initial 130 ships, over a third failed to return.

During this period, Elizabethan seamanship became renowned and the defeat of the Spanish confirmed English naval expertise and power.

But this was not enough for the Elizabethans; they were now increasingly setting sail on voyages of discovery, which saw England start to emerge as a global power. Between 1577 and 1580, Sir Francis Drake, partially sponsored by the Queen, took to the oceans in his ship the *Pelican*.

Today there is a replica of the Golden Hind, *which sits on the south bank of the River Thames. The original was known for her circumnavigation of the globe between 1577 and 1580. Drake renamed the* Pelican *mid-voyage in 1578, in honour of his patron and sponsor Sir Christopher Hatton, whose crest was a golden 'hind' (a female red deer).*

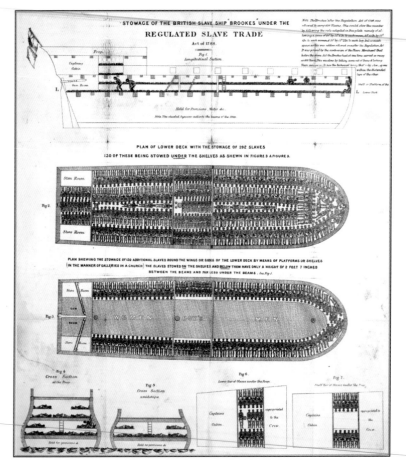

This diagram of the Brookes *slave ship was probably the most powerful image used by abolitionist campaigners. It shows the ship loaded to its full capacity, with 454 poor unfortunates crammed into the hold.*

The Slave Trade

This was a despicable and hugely profitable business that began in the 16th century. The trading ships, as they were called, set sail from Europe with a cargo of manufactured goods, heading for the west coast of Africa. Once they arrived, over the weeks and months that followed these goods would be traded for people captured by African traders. These intermediaries raided settlements far away from the African coast and brought young, healthy captives to the ports to be sold as slaves.

The deck of a slaveship showing the stern, the lower part of a mast and sail, 1792. The conditions that slaves were held in were barbaric, with hideous punishments used to enforce a vile regime upon those who had in truth been kidnapped.

Once a ship was packed, literally, full of slaves, they would set sail once more and head for the notorious 'Middle Passage', the established routes for slave ships from the west coast of Africa to the Americas and the Caribbean. After a further transatlantic journey back to their original points of departure, they would begin the cycle again by loading up with cargoes of sugar, rum, tobacco and other 'luxury' items. By 1790, it is estimated that 480,000 people were enslaved in the British colonies. In 1807, Great Britain made the slave trade illegal, and in 1833 it abolished slavery altogether.

Other business

While the Tudor navy had been a great success, the early Stuart period saw things deteriorate, mainly through poor investment and corruption during what became a prolonged period of peace. Naval expeditions were poorly organized and often ended in disaster with numerous people dying of sickness and disease.

Under James I, things began to improve with nine new ships being built and then, during the early part of Charles I's reign, the Navy had new ambitions, the royal fleet now being funded by the unpopular 'Ship Money' tax of 1637 – this tax was imposed intermittently by the Kingdom of England up until the middle of the 17th century.

Foisted upon the inhabitants of coastal areas, it was one of several taxes that English monarchs could charge by entitlement and without the approval of Parliament. Through this tax, three new ships were built, including the first three-gun-deck warship *Sovereign of the Seas* of 1637, which, after a rebuild in 1660, influenced the future design of later 'First Rates' of 100 guns – a First Rate was the designation for the largest ships of the line, which included the *Britannia* in 1682 and *Victory*, launched in 1737.

HMS Britannia *seen in two positions – broadside and stern.*

In January 1642, Parliament took control of the Navy and, while both sides did battle at sea during the Civil War, the fact that the Navy had sided with Parliament against the Crown was one of the decisive factors in the struggle.

Although seven frigates were constructed between 1645 and 1647 – a Parliamentary Commission for the Admiralty ordered further new ships – the frigates were seen as lacking in 'accommodation for men of war'. The Commission also introduced the original 'Articles of War', a set of regulations drawn up to govern the conduct of a country's military and naval forces.

It did not take long for Parliament to understand just how powerful the Navy could be, and soon they set the fleet on their commercial rivals, the Dutch. While the English Civil War was taking place, the Netherlands was busy securing its position as a powerful commercial rival to England, particularly in the Far East through its own East India Company.

Far left: *Maarten Harpertszoon Tromp, an officer and later admiral in the Dutch navy.*

Left: *Admiral Robert Blake was one of the most important military commanders of the Commonwealth of England in the 17th century.*

The Skirmish of Goodwin Sands, *19 May 1652*.

To protect its position in North America, the English Parliament passed the first of the Navigation Acts in October 1651, which meant that all goods imported to England had to be carried aboard English ships. In response to this growing intimidation, the Dutch procured large numbers of armed merchantmen for their navy.

The English, believing that they should be seen as the 'Lords of the Seas', tried to bring back an ancient regulation that required ships of other nations to lower their flags in deference to English vessels, even in foreign ports. On 19 May 1652, Lieutenant-Admiral Maarten Tromp refused to lower the Dutch flag. This led to a skirmish – the Battle of Goodwin Sands – after which the Commonwealth declared war on 10 July, leading to the first three Anglo–Dutch Wars (1652–74).

The Battle of Solebay (1672) off the Suffolk coast marked the start of the third Dutch war. Here, the English suffered, among other setbacks, the loss of their newest and largest ship, the 100-gun First Rate *Royal James*.

In 1706, the Navy introduced an approved standardization for the dimensions of each rate of warship. This was intended to establish a template for the design of ships for the foreseeable future.

The burning of the Royal James *at the Battle of Solebay, 7 June 1672. De Ruyter's flagship,* De Zeven Provinciën, *is shown in the left background. It is in close combat with Sir Joseph Jordan on* Royal Sovereign. *The ship to the right of the* Royal James *is that of Vice-Admiral Johan de Liefde.*

The Battle of Quiberon Bay was a conclusive naval battle fought near St Nazaire on 20 November between the Royal Navy and the French navy. It's where a British fleet of 24 ships engaged a French fleet of 21 ships. It was a tough battle, but in the end the British fleet sank or ran aground six French ships, captured one and scattered the rest. Victory meant the end of the threat of French invasion.

A new Dublin class gunship (the first 74-gun ships to be designed for the Royal Navy) was ordered in 1755. With this, the Admiralty achieved the greatest breakthrough in British naval shipbuilding in the 18th century. These vessels took part in the capture of Quebec and helped destroy the French fleet under the command of General Wolfe in Quiberon Bay. These ships set the example for the other class of vessels of the line, which included the 100-gun *Victory*.

In this illustration, HMS Agamemnon *can be seen on the left battling with* Ça Ira *on 13 March 1795. Nelson served as* Agamemnon's *captain from January 1793 for three years and three months.*

Trafalgar

By 1763, the 74s had become the backbone of the Navy, but by now the fleet was thinly spread across the world, guarding colonies in America, the Caribbean and India, while also defending British interests in almost every ocean. A cheaper 64-gun ship was being developed, to be used for convoy escort, patrol and amphibious duties. Thirty-three examples of this class were built between 1763 and 1780, including Nelson's favourite ship, the *Agamemnon*.

In Europe, the most powerful land power in 1805 was the First French Empire under Napoleon Bonaparte, although Britain's Royal Navy was in control of the seas and had imposed a naval blockade on France, which restricted Gallic movement of trade and any ability to mobilize their navy.

Napoleon, always one to expand his horizons, was determined to defeat the British, and so the two enemies found themselves constantly in hot pursuit of each other. The crunch finally came when they met at Cape Trafalgar off the coast of south-west Spain on 21 October 1805. The infamous battle that ensued took place between the Royal Navy and France backed up by its ally Spain.

The Royal Navy, commanded by Admiral Horatio Nelson, had 27 ships, while the French and Spanish forces, commanded by Admiral Pierre de Villeneuve, had 33, which left the British somewhat outnumbered.

Battle commenced with the French and Spanish ships all lined up in a row, but Nelson decided that rather than line up against them he would attack by forming two columns of ships, with the aim of pushing through enemy lines and splitting up their ships into smaller groups.

Inset: *Pierre-Charles-Jean-Baptiste-Silvestre de Villeneuve was a French naval officer during the Napoleonic Wars and commanded the French and Spanish fleets that were defeated by Nelson at the Battle of Trafalgar.*

Main image: *Lord Nelson, who died at Trafalgar, is depicted on the right.*

At the start of the battle, using naval flags, Nelson sent out a signal from his ship, HMS *Victory*. It said: 'England expects that every man will do his duty.' Soon the Royal Navy succeeded in penetrating the enemy line and after a fierce battle between the two navies, the battle came to an end at 4.30 pm as the last of the French and Spanish forces surrendered or were overwhelmed.

The Battle of Trafalgar, 21 October 1805 *is an 1822 painting by British artist J. M. W. Turner. This was commissioned by King George IV as a part of a series to decorate three state reception rooms in St James's Palace, with the aim of linking the Hanoverian dynasty to military success.*

Painter Denis Dighton's interpretation of Nelson lying wounded on the quarter-deck of HMS Victory.

Although it was a great victory for the Royal Navy, a total of 8,500 men were killed and wounded, one being Lord Nelson himself. He was shot and died of his wounds in the closing stages of the battle. But this extraordinary triumph over the combined Franco-Spanish fleet ensured Britain's protection from invasion for the remainder of the Napoleonic Wars.

Main image: *HMS* Victory *in a Portsmouth dry dock.*

The rear end of Victory.

Top: *Just two of the 104 guns that* Victory *carried.* Below: *A section on one side of* Victory *showing the gun ports and their flaps.*

French and British ships battling on Chesapeake Bay, 3 September 1781, during the American Revolutionary War. Opposite: HMS Trincomalee.

Revolution

The American Revolutionary War, aka the American War of Independence (1775–1783), was fought between the British and its 13 colonies. The outcome saw the colonies declare independence and become the United States of America. Conducting war on a number of different fronts, the Navy found itself dangerously stretched, with orders for new ships peaking in 1782.

But by now the Treasury had exhausted its funds with all the demands of the previous four years. Timber was now scarce and with the naval threat from France pretty much eliminated, fewer ships were being built. Many warships were laid up, scrapped or converted into prisons and stores.

Launched in 1817, the Trincomalee was built in Bombay, India. Unusually, she is made from teak, due to chronic oak shortages in Britain following the Napoleonic Wars. After being fitted out, Trincomalee was placed in reserve until 1845, at which time she was re-armed with fewer guns but more firepower. It seems that not only single passengers travelled on board but whole families, who shared sleeping arrangements. If for some reason you died, they would wrap you in a hammock, place a cannon ball at your feet and throw you overboard. It wasn't advisable to keep dead bodies on board for long periods!

Above: *Hoisting the flag: Admiral Arthur Phillip was the first Governor of New South Wales; he founded the British penal colony that later became the city of Sydney.*

Right: *In 1770, explorer James Cook mapped the east coast of Australia, naming it New South Wales and claiming it for Great Britain.*

Convict ships

In the view of the ruling classes of the 18th century, even minor criminals had to be separated from the rest of the community. This led to criminals either being exiled or killed. To imprison them in jails at home was far too expensive.

At first, criminals were sent to America, but after the country gained independence in the Revolutionary War, they refused to take any more, and so another place had to be found. Bearing in mind the notion that French colonial expansion could be nipped in the bud at the same time, Britain chose Australia for its convicts. The First Fleet set sail from Britain in 1787 and arrived in Botany Bay between 18 and 20 January 1788, where they established a penal colony in New South Wales. This land had been claimed for Britain by explorer James Cook on his first voyage to the Pacific in 1770.

HMS Endeavour, *a British Royal Navy research vessel that Lieutenant James Cook commanded to Australia and New Zealand on his first voyage of discovery from 1768 to 1771.*

During the hellish six months it took to get to the Antipodes – the criminals were chained up on the lower deck – nearly ten per cent of those who took the voyage died. Not in fact a bad percentage when you consider subsequent numbers. Later journeys saw nearer one third of the criminals die.

Present on this first voyage were seamen, marines and their families, government officials, and a large number of convicts – 582 men, 193 women and 14 children. Most were British, but African, American and French convicts were also on board. The type of crimes that they had committed were: petty theft – by far the most common offence; burglary or housebreaking; highway robbery; stealing clothing or animals; military offences; prostitution and crimes of deception.

The First Fleet enters Port Jackson in January 1788.

Left: Success *was a convict ship. After trading around the Indian subcontinent, she was sold to London owners and made three voyages with 'emigrants' to Australia during the 1840s.*

Right: *If you misbehaved on the voyage you could be put in this fearsome contraption – the wooden maiden. Inside this coffin-like enclosure, clad in iron, there was no light and nails protruded from the walls in case you decided to fall asleep. It was inhumane but commanded no little respect.* (Below) *Torture irons on* Success.

Black-eyed Sue and Sweet Poll of Plymouth take leave of their lovers who are on their way to Botany Bay. A jailer with a pistol in his belt standing behind the women points sternly to a ship in the background. On a distant hill in the background, a body dangles from a tiny gibbet.

Once in Australia, criminals were not kept behind bars, but put to work; most experienced an extremely tough life. Sadistic guards were happy to dish out punishment and 100 lashes from the cat-o'-nine-tails persuaded most to toe the line. It was said that blood was usually drawn after five lashes and convicts ended up walking home in boots filled with their own blood – if they could manage to walk at all, that is. The *Hougoumont* was the last convict ship to make the journey and it arrived in Western Australia in 1868. Between 1788 and 1868, 608 convict ships transported more than 162,000 convicts to Australia.

The Macquarie Harbour Penal Station was established on Sarah Island in the former colony of Van Diemen's Land, now Tasmania. It was in operation between 1822 and 1833. The settlement housed mainly male convicts, with a small number of women. During this time, the colony achieved a reputation as one of the harshest penal settlements in Australia.

2 Full Steam Ahead

The Victorian Era (1837–1901)

Alexandrina Victoria became Queen of the United Kingdom of Great Britain and Ireland on 20 June 1837. Just one month later, Isambard Kingdom Brunel launched his revolutionary steamship the *Great Western* at Bristol.

Only a year earlier, in 1836, Brunel and his friend Thomas Guppy, along with a group of Bristol investors, created the Great Western Steamship Company. They were progressive thinkers and one of the subjects under discussion at the time was a regular scheduled transatlantic service. Their aim was to build a line of steamships specifically designed for the Bristol to New York sea route.

The coronation of Queen Victoria.

The *Great Western* featured an iron-strapped, wooden-hull design, with paddles on either side of the decks. She also had four masts, with sails that could provide added propulsion in bad weather, helping to keep the paddles turning over in rough water. After construction, she sailed to London, where she was fitted with two side-lever steam engines – the largest ever built up to that time. Her design caused controversy, with many critics commenting that she was too big, but she was able to demonstrate the benefits of steam over sails for transatlantic travel, and paved the way for future Atlantic paddle-steamers.

Above: *The* Great Western. (Right) *The classic photograph of Brunel in front of massive anchor chains belonging to the SS* Great Eastern *at a shipyard in Millwall.*

The Charlotte Dundas.

From 1837 to 1839, she was the largest passenger ship in the world and made a record number of Blue Riband trips up to 1843. After eight years of working the New York route, her owners went out of business and she was sold to the Royal Mail Steam Packet Company. She served as a troop ship during the Crimean War and was scrapped in 1856.

Considered to be the first practical steam boat, the *Charlotte Dundas*, built in 1802, preceded Brunel's designs by some 30 years, when she managed to tow two 70-ton barges along the Forth and Clyde Canal. With further development of boiler and cylinder design, the Clyde-based paddle steamer (PS) *Comet* proved to be the first commercially successful steam boat service in 1812. These vessels, which rolled off the production line, were used predominantly on river estuaries where the water was fairly still. Because they didn't have to rely on the wind, they were able to keep to regular schedules.

The Comet *was Europe's first successful steam-powered passenger vessel. She served Greenock, Helensburgh and Glasgow for two centuries of steaming and ferrying up, down and across the River Clyde in Scotland. This replica of the* Comet *can be seen at Port Glasgow.*

CHAPTER 2

Paddle power

The PS *Margery* was part of a regular ferry service along the Thames from 1815, and by 1821 the first steam-powered cross-Channel service commenced. With steam now proving itself, the 1820s saw new shipyards in London producing steamboats for services and routes along the coasts. This was soon extended to include longer journeys to far-flung outposts such as the Far East. The one big drawback steam had was the amount of fuel needed, which on long journeys not only took up space on board ships but time to deliver, too.

The Royal Navy was reluctant initially to adopt steam-powered ships; their first was HMS *Comet*, launched at Deptford in 1822. She was commissioned as a tug for towing ships, in particular

Henry Bell was the owner of a hotel and baths in Helensburgh. To be able to transport his customers across the Clyde, he commissioned his own ship named Comet. *At the time, a 'best cabin' cost four shillings (maybe £100 in today's money).*

Comet's *paddles can be seen here underneath their housing.*

The plaque in Port Glasgow that celebrates the making and launch of this historical boat.

HM ships stuck in the Thames Medway when the wind was not strong enough to pull them out of harbour. Wooden hulls also took a while to be phased out, but with the availability of iron and new rolling mills, in conjunction with the rising cost of timber, minds were changed. The directors of the Great Western Steamship Company decided that they would build an even larger and faster ship than the *Great Western*, and so the keel of the SS *Great Britain* was laid down in 1839. She combined two innovative features: she was built of iron and equipped with a screw propeller, the first large ocean-going ship to have one. She was also the first iron steamer to cross the Atlantic in 1845, in just 14 days. The Admiralty may have been slow to see the potential of steam power, but by 1837 they too had succumbed and had 37 steam-powered vessels on the books.

The SS Great Britain.

Top: *The ornate rear of the SS* Great Britain. *Left: The SS* Great Britain *was the first ship to cross the Atlantic with a screw propeller.*
Below: *The massive engine attached to the rudder and propeller at the rear of the ship.*

Rattling along

Paddle propulsion would also soon be phased out in the Navy, after a celebrated towing contest was held between the screw-driven HMS *Rattler* and paddle frigate HMS *Alecto*. The result saw *Rattler* tow *Alecto* astern at a speed of 2.8 knots.

The change from paddle to screw propulsion happened over a 20-year period, with companies like Cunard ordering paddle steamers as late as the 1860s. During the Industrial Revolution, England had large supplies of iron ore and coal, thus allowing it to produce an abundance of items made from metal, including engines, at a much cheaper price than its competitors. A wide variety of steam engines was developed during this period. One example that has survived using a single-cylinder engine is the drag-boat *Bertha*. Built in 1844, she was used to remove silt from the Port of Bridgwater in Somerset. She is the oldest operational steam vessel in Britain and possibly the world.

The Crimean War – fought against the declining Ottoman Empire from 1853 to 1856 – is seen by many as the first modern war, due to the use of what were then new technologies: electric telegraphy and the railways. While the Allies, Britain, France, Turkey and the Kingdom of Sardinia were successful in their naval campaign, it became obvious that wooden-hulled vessels were extremely vulnerable to fire from modern, shore-based artillery. The French used iron cladding to protect their ships, an idea that quickly caught on with the Royal Navy. The Aetna-class ironclad floating batteries, as they became known, were built to attack Russian coastal fortifications. The British planned to use their batteries in the Baltic Sea against Kronstadt in 1856, which resulted in the Russians suing for peace. These iron-armoured batteries could also be seen as early steps towards the development of ironclad warships and finally the battleship.

The Admiralty ordered the building of two ironclads, the *Warrior* and *Black Prince* in 1859, which were the most powerful fighting ships in the world at the time; they also changed the balance of naval power.

HMS Warrior *was a 40-gun, steam-powered, armoured frigate, built for the Royal Navy in 1859–61 and was the name ship of the Warrior-class ironclads.*

Along with her sister ship HMS Black Prince, HMS Warrior (pictured here) was the first armour-plated, iron-hulled warship.

The new breed of boats

Soon even these two ironclads would be overshadowed and, as technology advanced, a submarine was developed and used during the American Civil War (1861–65).

There had been designs and ideas for submarines prior to this, but it was in 1864 that the Confederate navy's *H. L. Hunley* became the first military submarine to sink an enemy vessel, the Union sloop-of-war USS *Housatonic*. Unfortunately, after the attack, the *Hunley* also sank, possibly due to being too close to the explosion.

Many of the advances in naval engineering were down to the mercantile community, who were always aware of the profits that could be made abroad. With increasing trade between Britain and Australia, Brunel put a proposition forward for a ship

The inventor of this submarine, H. L. Hunley, is depicted next to his boat along with a sentinel. This was a submarine of the Confederate States of America, a footnote in the American Civil War. The Confederacy lost 21 crewmen in three sinkings of Hunley *during her short career.*

that could travel to Australia and back without having to coal-up. The ship that resulted was the *Leviathan* – the original name of the *Great Eastern* – launched in 1858.

The Great Eastern *under construction at Millwall.*

The Great Eastern *docked in New York City, with a Western Hotel coach and people on the dock.*

Main image: *Colour print of the* Great Eastern *after a painting by Edwin Weedon.*

The *Great Eastern* was the biggest ship of her time and she could carry up to 4,000 passengers. Brunel affectionately called her the 'Great Babe'. Sadly, he died shortly after her ill-fated maiden voyage during which she was damaged by an explosion. She was repaired and travelled between Britain and North America, after which she was converted to a cable-laying vessel – laying the first transatlantic telegraph cable in 1866. She finished her days as a floating billboard and music hall in Liverpool and was broken up in 1889. One of her funnels – she originally had five, later reduced to four – is displayed at the SS *Great Britain* Museum in Bristol.

The Great Eastern *seen at the end of her life as a floating billboard and music hall in Liverpool.*

The demand for coal seemed endless and, by 1844, 2.5 million tons was shipped annually to London in 9,500 separate voyages, with the volume increasing year on year up to the turn of the century. Ships were now mainly made of iron, and the shipbuilding industry had to up sticks and move. Once predominantly in the south of England, the industry headed north, where raw materials and mechanical skills required for metal-hulled ships were cheaper. Places like Clydeside, Merseyside, Tyneside and the coast of Durham, where coal was abundant and the docks were sheltered, were chosen. By 1860, the number of ships being built was astounding, with 178 vessels being produced on the Clyde alone. One of these was the *Iona II*, a paddle steamer that was fitted out with twin-cylinder engines and other modern features. She was initially seen as a luxury steamer, but because of her speed she was acquired as a blockade runner to take guns and supplies to the Confederate forces during the American Civil War. Sadly, she never made it as far as America, sinking in bad weather off Lundy Island, Devon.

An iron-hulled paddle steamer, Iona II, *was built in 1863 on the river Clyde. Clyde steamers were well-known for their creature comforts, but* Iona II *was way ahead of the field. There was space available for both cabin and steerage passengers to dine, wash and walk in surroundings that matched whatever prices they could afford.*

Clippers

Even in the 1860s, long-distance cargo carrying was still dominated by sailing ships, with steam playing a secondary role; nothing, it seemed, could match the legendary clipper ships. These had no fuel bills or mechanical breakdowns and crews were smaller. An example of this was the *Cutty Sark*, which was built in 1869 and designed to transport luxury goods, such as tea and wool, from far-off places such as China and Australia.

The Cutty Sark *moored in Melbourne, Australia. At least one other clipper can be seen in the background.*

Today Cutty Sark *is a museum ship and you can find it in Greenwich, London.*

79

The passing of peak sail

The 1860s was a peak period for long-distance sailing ships, but the opening of the Suez Canal in 1869 meant that steam began to take over. By using the canal, travel times to places like India and the Far East were cut considerably; at the same time, the canal was not suitable for sailing vessels due to wind direction. Another key factor was the introduction of the compound engine, an important development in marine engineering. These engines gave fuel savings of up to 40 per cent, allowing more space for cargo. The number of ships fitted with this type of engine trebled between 1870 and 1875, with the final total surpassing 2,000 vessels.

Docking with due care and attention. This is the White Star liner Oceanic *parking up in New York.*

The Oregon *was a record-breaking British passenger liner that won the Blue Riband for the Guion Line as the fastest liner on the Atlantic in 1884. She was sold to the Cunard Line. Her demise came when she collided with a schooner while approaching New York.*

Many countries now used 'liners', which transported people and goods on a particular route at specific times. Large companies now sprang up and took over the reins – Cunard, White Star, the P&O Company and Union Castle. Some just transported people, but others brought in a mix of goods and passengers.

So-called long-distance 'tramp steamers' worked a variety of routes depending on their cargo; new destinations could be conveyed to them by telegraphy and later by radio. Soon ships were being built for specific cargoes, thus bringing into being coasters, grain ships, refrigeration ships, cattle ships, whale factory ships and cable-laying ships. Britain played a leading role in developing, constructing and managing these enterprises.

The coaster SS *Robin* is a survivor of this period and the only complete example of a coastal cargo steamer still left, as well as being the oldest complete steamship. She was built in Bow Creek, London in 1890 and, although built for British owners, she spent most of her long working life along the Spanish coast under the name of *Maria*.

The SS Robin *museum, theatre and educational centre, as she is now known, went through extensive renovation within and without. She now sits proudly at the western end of the Royal Victoria Dock, London.*

The RNLI

Ships were becoming bigger and existing docks struggled to accommodate these new supersized steel monsters. Southampton docks opened in 1843 and was used extensively by the P&O Line. Southampton took over from London as the major transoceanic passenger port and was used for the embarkation of passengers and goods, with the White Star Line and American Star Line quickly transferring there. In 1876, the Merchant Shipping Act was announced, which raised shipping standards by law. A major force was Samuel Plimsoll, who introduced what became known as the Plimsoll line – ships were banned from loading if it meant the water level went above the line. Other legislation enforced better standards for crew members and in 1824 a lifeboat service was created, later to become the Royal National Lifeboat Institution (RNLI).

The memorial to Samuel Plimsoll on Victoria Embankment, London.

Birnbeck Pier is situated in the Bristol Channel, off Weston-super-Mare. Because of the remarkable tidal range found along there, the Royal National Lifeboat Institution (RNLI) had difficulty in finding the right place to launch their lifeboats from. In 1882, davits were installed on the pier and this allowed the lifeboats to be lowered and launched into the water below. The pier also became a boarding point for steamers plying their trade in the Bristol Channel. The final excursion visited the pier in 1979.

Below left: *The* Alfred Corry *lifeboat constructed in 1893. Launched in anger 41 times, she is credited with saving 47 lives during her 15-year career.*

Below right: *Poster for the Royal National Lifeboat Institution, 1914.*

ROYAL NATIONAL
LIFEBOAT INSTITUTION
Supported solely by Voluntary Contributions
PATRONS:— THEIR MAJESTIES THE KING AND QUEEN
HER MAJESTY QUEEN ALEXANDRA
OUR WORK IN 1914

In the Year
LIVES-1,112-SAVED

In a Month
LIVES-239-SAVED

In a Week
LIVES-173-SAVED

In a Day
LIVES-152-SAVED

1824 to 1914
TOTAL 52.526 SAVED

HMS *Devastation*

By 1876, the number of steamships outnumbered those under sail, and after the 1880s, steel began to replace iron in both warships and merchant shipping. Using steel construction meant reducing the dimensions of all parts of the hull. With the introduction of the self-propelled torpedo by the Royal Navy came new specialist light craft such as the 'torpedo boat'. To counter this threat, a new type of ship was introduced in 1880, the 'torpedo-boat destroyer', or simply destroyer as we know it today.

Sail was now outdated and a new ship, the *Devastation* (seen below), was commissioned in

1873. It was the first of two Devastation-class mastless turret ships built for the Royal Navy. It was also the first to place the entire main armament mounted on top of the hull rather than inside it. While this seemed to mark the end of the sailing warship, the Royal Navy still introduced HMS *Gannet* – see overleaf. Classed as a screw sloop and the last of the Victorian 'gunboats'. She was sent overseas to police the British Empire trade routes until 1895. The main objective for ships like the *Gannet* was to maintain British naval dominance through trade protection, anti-slavery vigilance, and long-term surveying.

HMS Gannet *was heavily armed. Among other weapons, three RML (Rifled Muzzle Loading) guns, like this one, were positioned on her main deck. This gun fired a shell that weighed 64 lbs (29 kg), which could reach a distance of nearly three miles (4.8 km).*

The huge success of the compound engine was followed in 1874 by the new and more powerful triple-expansion engine. Again, the savings in coal allowed the ships to be larger, paving the way for transatlantic liners such as the British-built *City of Paris* – the first ship to make the crossing in fewer than six days – and the *City of New York*, which made its bow in 1888.

USS City of New York, *an ocean-liner steamship.*

Opposite: *HMS* Hood. Below: *The SS* City of Paris, *which was later known simply as* Paris.

Also fitted with triple-expansion engines were the Royal Sovereign-class battleships – at the time, the most powerful battleships in the world. HMS *Hood* (above) was built for the Royal Navy in the early 1890s, but differed slightly from the others in the class. She was used in the development of anti-torpedo bulges in 1913 and not long afterwards, at the start of World War I, she was scuttled. This saw her acting as a blockship across the southern entrance of Portland harbour against any possible U-boat torpedo attacks.

The quadruple-expansion marine engine was next to make its debut and, although the most powerful of its time, it was relatively short-lived when the piston-driven engines were rendered obsolete by the steam turbine. The *Turbinia* was launched in 1894, initially as an experimental vessel, and was not only the first to be driven by a steam turbine engine, but also easily the fastest ship in the world at this time.

Left: Turbinia *seen at speed, and below is the Parsons Radial-Flow steam turbine engine that powered her.*

The Golden Age of Ocean Travel

1901–1923

RMS *Victorian* and RMS *Virginian*, although they later sailed under different names, belonged to the British-owned Allan Line. These liners were launched in 1904 and were the first large civilian ships to be propelled by steam turbines. In 1907 these were followed by the Royal Mail Ship the *Mauretania* and RMS *Lusitania*, and with this the Golden Age of ocean travel began in earnest; everything was better in terms of speed, comfort and size.

The main image shows the Mauretania steaming at a leisurely pace.

Left: *People watching games on the deck of the Mauretania, c. 1911.*

Windjammers

Even though significant advances had been made with marine power-plants, the era of sailing ships was by no means over. Windjammers, as they were known, were large merchant sailing ships, equipped with between three and five tall masts and square sails. They were the last breed of large commercial sailing vessel, designed using scientific methods and modern materials such as iron and steel in their construction. The cargo that these workhorses transported all around the globe varied widely – from lumber, guano and grain to iron ore and other raw materials – and they travelled unceasingly between continents.

The *Balclutha* was built in 1886 in Scotstoun, Glasgow. She was designed as a general trading vessel and rounded Cape Horn 17 times in 13 years, ferrying such cargoes as wine, case oil and coal from Europe and the United States to ports in the Pacific.

Originally christened Euterpe *after the muse of music,* The Star of India *was built at Ramsey in the Isle of Man in 1863 to serve the Indian jute trade. She then did 25 years of hard graft, carrying British emigrants to New Zealand and ended up as a salmon hauler on the Alaska–California run, retiring in 1926. She was refitted in 1962-63 and resumed her working life with the Maritime Museum in San Diego.*

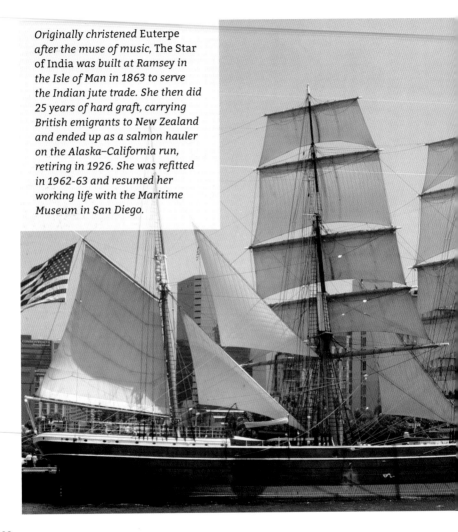

Top and above: The five-masted Preußen *['Prussia'] was the largest windjammer ever built, measuring 5,081 Gross Registered Tonnage (GRT).*

RRS *Discovery*

RRS *Discovery* is a barque-rigged auxiliary steamship, which was built for Antarctic research; she was launched in 1901. Less than five months later, she set sail on the British National Antarctic Expedition. Her sea trials were short and sweet, but it seems her speed under steam was better than expected. Due to the lack of available crew and the limited time between build and setting off, neither her builder nor Captain Scott were able to assess her ability under sailing conditions. And neither Scott nor Shackleton seemed to take to the vessel, pointing out several negative features. But as the voyage towards the Antarctic continued, the ship proved its seaworthiness. They finally sighted the Antarctic coastline on 8 January 1902.

RRS Discovery *was the last wooden three-masted ship to be built in the UK. She can now be seen at Discovery Point, Dundee, the city where she was built.*

Stepping on the gas

Another major step was taken in 1870, when oil from the Caspian Sea became an alternative for coal-burning vessels. The advantages allowed a ship to travel further and at higher speeds for the same weight of coal. It also reduced bunkering time and the number of stokers required. It took a while for coal stations to be replaced, due to the number of ships using the material, but by 1911 oil-bunkering stations were widely available. The Acheron-class destroyers of the Royal Navy were all oil-burners from that year on.

The widespread use of submarines didn't really come about until the early 1900s and this became a key time for their development, along with other technological advancements. Diesel-electric power was now used to propel submarines and periscopes were a standard fit. Experiments with tactics and weapons were carried out and all this had a huge impact on their use during World War I.

Holland 1, *often referred to as HM submarine Torpedo Boat No 1, was the first submarine commissioned by the Royal Navy in 1900.*

Further advances were made when the Italian inventor Guglielmo Marconi successfully transmitted radio signals across the English Channel in 1898. By 1901, ship-to-shore communication was tested effectively when the British ship *Lake Champlain* successfully connected with a shore-based radio station on the Isle of Wight.

A view inside Holland 1 *showing her torpedo tube.*

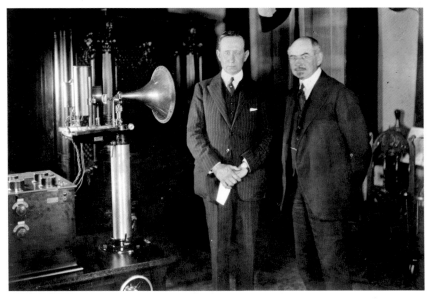

Italian inventor Guglielmo Marconi (left) with electrical pioneer Edwin Wilbur Rice, Jr., one of the three founders of General Electric.

The *Titanic*

The disaster that befell RMS *Titanic* in April 1912 saw two of the crew, Jack Phillips and Harold Bride, remain at their station until the last moment transmitting distress signals. The *Titanic* hit an iceberg in the North Atlantic and five of the ship's watertight compartments were ruptured. She started sinking bow-first, with water pouring in from one compartment to the next as the tilt became more acute. After the boat sank, some 710 people managed to survive and be rescued by the *Carpathia* for transportation to New York. Sadly, at least 1,500 people lost their lives, mostly from cardiac arrest due to the freezing cold water – *Carpathia*'s captain described the area as an ice field.

The 'unsinkable' RMS Titanic departing from Southampton on 10 April 1912.

Opposite (anti-clockwise): Belfast, 31 May 1911 – the huge propeller of the Titanic *dwarfs the workers preparing to watch her launch; the immense structure of the* Titanic *takes shape – the sheer size of the ship proved a major engineering challenge for builders Harland and Wolff; onboard entertainment – the veranda cafe and palm court of the* Titanic.

Below: *Not a great way to become famous, but Ned Parfett was known as the 'Titanic paperboy'. In this film still, he is shown on the day they announced the disaster – 16 April 1912.*

Above: *Harold Bride, surviving wireless operator of the* Titanic, *is carried up the ramp of a homebound ship, his frostbitten feet in bandages.*

Kaiser Wilhelm II in 1902.   *Admiral Alfred von Tirpitz.*

This cover of Puck features a high-stakes poker game between Uncle Sam, German Emperor Wilhelm II, Meiji, Emperor of Japan, Emile Loubet, of France, and Edward VII, King of Great Britain. The Emperor of Japan is raising the bidding by one battleship.

Arms race

It's probably mostly forgotten now, but there was an arms race between the United Kingdom and the German Empire from the last decade of the 19th century through to the start of World War I in 1914. German Admiral Alfred von Tirpitz decided in 1897 to create a naval fleet large enough to force Britain to make diplomatic concessions. Because of the strength and size of the Royal Navy, Tirpitz did not expect the Imperial German Navy to be able to defeat it. And so, with the backing of Kaiser Wilhelm II, Tirpitz ordered an increased number of surface warships.

In the meantime, the construction of HMS *Dreadnought* in 1906 (see opposite) – the first major warship to be turbine driven – prompted Tirpitz to escalate his building programme, which in turn saw the Royal Navy step up the construction of more Dreadnoughts. The arms race was well and truly under way. After 1912, mainly due to the costs involved, Germany decided on a policy of detente with Britain.

Dreadnought was followed in 1912 by HMS *Bristol*, which was the first warship to run on superheated steam (from its 12 boilers). This gave her superior speed along with better fuel economy.

But war now seemed inevitable and in 1914 the action kicked off; by early 1915, the waters around the British Isles had been declared a war zone. By September of that year, some 480 merchant vessels had been sunk by German U-boats, which included the Cunard liner the *Lusitania*. On 7 May, she was torpedoed off the Irish coast, with a loss of 1,201 men, women and children.

Left: *The poster speaks for itself.*

Below: *Happy Days – the* Lusitania *arrives at the Cunard dock in New York after a record-breaking journey.*

A drawing, made for the New York Herald *and the* London Sphere, *showing the RMS* Lusitania *at the moment a second torpedo strikes the hull.*

Although anti-submarine tactics were being employed by the Royal Navy, they were basic. By 1916, the Allies were losing some 65 merchant ships for every enemy submarine, a figure that increased to 167 in 1917. Finally, though, a convoy system was introduced.

There were many naval confrontations during the war, but the largest battle at sea was Jutland. Britain's Royal Navy Grand Fleet was commanded by Admiral Sir John Jellicoe and the Imperial German Navy's High Seas Fleet came under the command of Vice-Admiral Reinhard Scheer. The Battle of Jutland was the only full-scale clash of battleships during the war.

It unfolded with extensive manoeuvring and three main engagements were fought between 31 May and 1 June 1916 off the North Sea coast of Denmark's Jutland peninsula. The aftermath of battle saw both sides claiming victory: the British lost more

Admiral Beatty.

Admiral Jellicoe.

Vice-Admiral Scheer.

This is the British battleship HMS Iron Duke, *the flagship of Admiral Sir John Jellicoe. As commander of the Grand Fleet, Jellicoe was in overall command of British ships during the Battle of Jutland. From the bridge of this ship, Jellicoe made critical tactical decisions.*

ships and twice as many sailors; however, they did manage to contain the German fleet.

Scheer's plan to destroy a significant portion of the British fleet also failed. The British long-term goal was to deny Germany access to both the United Kingdom and the Atlantic, which they managed to accomplish. In total, 8,000 sailors were killed and 25 ships were sunk. After the battle, the British press criticized the Grand Fleet's failure to force a decisive outcome and later Royal Navy enquiries produced varying judgments on the performance of the two home admirals, Jellicoe and Beatty. A debate over their performance in battle continues to this day.

Aircraft carriers

Initial experiments for launching and landing aircraft from ships started in the early 20th century, but HMS *Ark Royal* is seen by most as the first modern aircraft carrier. Originally designed as a merchant ship, she was then developed into a hybrid aeroplane/seaplane carrier with a launch platform. HMS *Furious* was also used during World War I as an experimental landing strip for aircraft. The first man to land his plane on a moving ship was Squadron Commander E. H. Dunning RN, who managed to land his Sopwith Pup on HMS *Furious* in Scapa Flow, Orkney on 2 August 1917. Sadly, he was killed just five days later attempting the same manoeuvre.

One of the most successful carrier operations of the war came on 19 July 1918 during the Tondern Raid. Launched from HMS *Furious*, seven Sopwith Camels, each armed with a pair of 50 lb bombs, attacked the German Zeppelin base at Tondern, Denmark. A number of airships and balloons were destroyed, but because *Furious* was unable to receive the returning aircraft, two had to ditch in the sea and the others made their way to neutral Denmark. This became the first ever carrier-launched strike.

HMS Furious in 1918, with palisade windbreaks raised on her flying-off deck, forward.

Above: *The first ship designed and built as a seaplane carrier, this is HMS* Ark Royal, *c. 1918.*

Right: *The flying-off deck of HMS* Furious *in 1918, looking forward from the bridge area. Seven Sopwith Camel aircraft are parked behind the ship's windbreaks.*

HMS M33 is an M29-class monitor of the Royal Navy. Built in 1915, she saw active service in World War I in the Mediterranean and was in Russia in 1919 during the Allied Intervention.

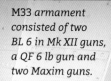

M33 *armament consisted of two BL 6 in Mk XII guns, a QF 6 lb gun and two Maxim guns.*

Top: *A convoy of ships during World War I –* Drake, Indomitable, Inflexible *and* Invincible.

Right: *The destruction of* HMS Queen Mary *during the Battle of Jutland.*

Opposite: *RMS* Viceroy of India.

After 7.7 million tons of British mercantile shipping had been lost during the war and needed replacing, shipyards and their workers were kept busy in the immediate post-war period. There were improvements to boilers and combustion chambers, along with innovations such as the introduction of electric drive for main propulsion. The first large British turbo-electric vessel was P&O's RMS *Viceroy of India*, which entered service in 1928. But the end of the war led to a downturn in shipping requirements, and this, together with the Wall Street Crash in 1929, meant there was less demand for shipping services. The lack of orders led to several shipbuilding yards closing across the United Kingdom – for example, the 15 yards on the Wear dwindled to six between 1921 and 1937. Demand would not pick up again in any substantial way until the onset of World War II.

4 War at Sea

1939 to 1945

Following the success of P&O's RMS *Viceroy of India*, Cunard were keen to respond and they came up with the RMS *Queen Mary*. This ship became a legend and took the Blue Riband in 1938, completing the Atlantic crossing in five days at an average speed of 30.99 knots. Her sister ship the *Queen Elizabeth* also provided weekly luxury liner services between Southampton and New York, via Cherbourg in France. Built in 1939, like the *Queen Mary*, she was used as a troop ship during World War II. These were seen as prestigious vessels with the best-quality fittings and the finest service; it was considered a privilege to travel on them.

Opposite: *RMS* Queen Mary *arriving in New York harbour, 20 June 1945, with thousands of US soldiers on board.*

This page: *Old meets new – a modern cruise liner sits at the rear of floating restaurant RMS* Queen Mary *in Long Beach, California.*

Above: Queen Mary's bridge – the captain's domain.

Left: A view from an upper deck looking forward and towards Long Beach. Below: The bandstand.

Left: Queen Mary *played her part in World War II, transporting troops, but she never encountered trouble.*

Above: *Wood panelling and comfortable surroundings in just one of several bars. Time to relax.*

Times were changing though and soon these beautiful liners and their passengers would be threatened with extinction by the new, much faster way of travelling – airliners in the sky.

Things were moving on, and a new type of engine was now being adopted, the diesel engine – named after Dr Rudolf Diesel. These engines were found to be more economical and higher speeds could be attained; the real advantages of the diesel engine would prove decisive in the second half of the 20th century when they were designed to work with 'residual' oil rather than the more expensive high-grade oil.

Up to 1939, the navies of the opposing powers had chosen the steam turbine as their choice of propulsion. HMS *Belfast* is a good example of this with her four Admiralty oil-fired, three-drum boilers and four Parsons single-reduction geared steam turbines. Launched in 1938, she is the largest surviving World War II warship in Europe, having done her bit during the fighting.

British light cruiser HMS Belfast *seen approaching USS* Bataan *while operating off the coast of Korea in 1952.*

Today HMS Belfast is moored on the Thames just up from Tower Bridge and is a tourist attraction run by the Imperial War Museum.

HMS Hood was one of the early casualties of World War II. Although well armed, she was hit several times and sank stern first (see next page). Of the 1,418 men on board, only three survived.

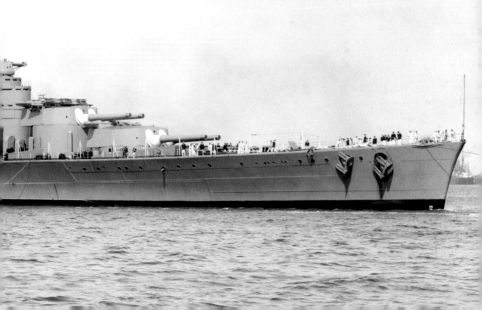

The carrier *Hermes*, the battleship *Prince of Wales*, the battlecruiser *Repulse* and the heavy cruisers *Exeter*, *Dorsetshire* and *Cornwall* were all lost in the Asian theatre.

A painting showing the sinking of HMS Hood *in battle with the German battleship* Bismark *on 24 May 1941. In the foreground is HMS* Prince of Wales, *later to become a casualty, too. The aircraft carriers* Hermes *(inset) and* Ark Royal *(below) were also destroyed.*

Above: *Dramatic scene showing passengers abandoning HMS* Courageous, *the British aircraft carrier, on 17 September 1939 after she was torpedoed by a German U-boat.*

Left: *Taken from a Japanese plane, this photo shows the* Prince of Wales *at far left and* Repulse *beyond her after the first torpedo attack.*

Estimates put the number of victims at between 3,000 and 5,800 when the converted troopship RMS *Lancastria* sank off Saint-Nazaire in June 1940 – the largest loss for a single ship in British maritime history.

The number of casualties aboard the Lancastria *was hushed up by Winston Churchill.*

Two weeks after Dunkirk, a packed *Lancastria*, the former Cunard cruise ship, was taking part in Operation Ariel, the hurried evacuation of British civilians and troops from France. *Lancastria* was bombed by Junkers Ju 88 German aircraft. She received three direct hits, then a fourth bomb fell down the ship's smokestack and detonated inside the engine room, releasing more than 1,200 tons of crude oil into the Loire estuary. Not long after the first hit, *Lancastria* capsized and German planes began strafing survivors in the water. *Lancastria* sank within twenty minutes.

Along with the losses, there were also some successes against enemy surface ships, for example the battles of the River Plate in 1939, Narvik in 1940 and Cape Matapan in 1941, and the sinking of the German capital ships *Bismarck* in 1941 and *Scharnhorst* in 1943.

Main image: *The cruisers HMS* Exeter *in the foreground and HMNZS* Achilles, *right centre background, in action against the famous German armoured ship* Admiral Graf Spee.

Above: *The German battleship* Bismarck *fires on HMS* Prince of Wales.

Opposite: *The German battleship* Scharnhorst.

Battle of the Atlantic

During what became known as the Battle of the Atlantic, the Germans used submarines to devastating effect, their aim being to cut Britain off from the world and starve it of essential supplies. While U-boats sank a huge number of ships, the convoys continued to travel back and forth across the Atlantic. Convoys featured from the start of the war and anti-submarine hunting patrols were organized, which saw the Royal Navy busy in the North Atlantic and Arctic oceans.

Nearer to home, the ports, harbours and sea-lanes around the coast became the responsibility of Coastal Forces and the Royal Naval Patrol Service. The Merchant Navy suffered huge losses, but along with the Royal Navy they kept the supply lines to the UK open for the transportation of food and other necessary goods.

A view showing just one of the many convoys that travelled across the dangerous waters of the Atlantic Ocean during World War II.

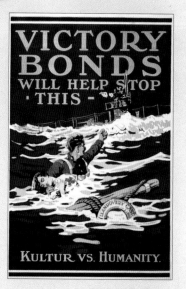

Main image: *In convoy, the men and guns of the naval vessels that protected British merchant convoys were ready for any emergency at any time. Here, a bluejacket keeps watch over ships plodding steadily across the Atlantic to bring vital supplies to Britain's allies and her far-flung battle fronts.*

Below: *Recruitment poster of the period.*

Inset: *Poster showing a Canadian soldier holding a drowned Red Cross worker and shaking his fist at sailors on a nearby German submarine. The poster refers to the sinking of the Canadian Red Cross transport ship, Llandovery Castle.*

Dunkirk

Following the invasion of northern Europe by Hitler's troops, tanks and aircraft, German forces trapped the British Expeditionary Forces (BEF), the remains of the Belgian forces, and three French field armies along the northern coast of France. Immediate evacuation across the Channel suddenly became the best course of action. This became known as Operation Dynamo, and later the Miracle of Dunkirk.

Allied troops on the beaches of Dunkirk try the best they can to defend themselves against attacks by German aircraft.

During the first day of the evacuation, some 7,669 Allied soldiers were repatriated and, by the end of the eighth day, a massive 338,226 had been rescued by a hastily assembled fleet of over 800 boats, which included 39 Royal Navy destroyers and four Royal Canadian Navy destroyers.

Allied soldiers escape to mainland England from the carnage at Dunkirk.

Soldiers were ferried not only to the larger ships, but also all the way back to mainland England by what became known as the 'little ships' of Dunkirk. These made up a flotilla of hundreds of merchant marine boats, fishing boats, pleasure craft, yachts and lifeboats, all of which had made the journey across the Channel from England to help evacuate the soldiers left behind on the French coast.

This image was taken during the 'Return to Dunkirk' for the 75th anniversary of Operation Dynamo, May 2015.

Little ships of Dunkirk

The main image shows the Princess Elizabeth, *named to celebrate the birth of Britain's current queen. In May 1940, she played a crucial part in Operation Dynamo. Accompanied by the other 'little ships', she sailed to Dunkirk to rescue the stranded soldiers. She alone saved 1,673 Allied soldiers in four crossings. Today, she can be seen at the Estacade Quay, Dunkirk harbour in France.*

Liberty ships

Because of the huge losses incurred during the early stages of World War II, merchant shipping needed to be replaced as quickly as possible. This led to standardization of power units, such as the triple-expansion engines; parts were now also being prefabricated and welded together rather than riveted, which reduced construction time. Vast numbers of these ships were being built by the USA and Canada, and they became known as Liberty ships. They weren't built for longevity, but they all contributed to final victory in the Battle of the Atlantic.

A line-up of British cargo-carrying ships built under lend-lease at a New England shipyard. They were due for baptism along with two destroyers and a Liberty ship at a record-breaking mass launching on 16 August 1942.

Birth of a ship. From keel laying to the launching ceremony, it took less than five months to build the Patrick Henry. *This was a record and construction time for sister ships of the Liberty Ship design soon came down to an average 42 days. This standard design was selected by the US Maritime Commission to meet the need for ships that could be built in existing yards in minimum time, with the additional purpose of conserving vital materials for the war effort. Prefabrication of sections in special plants, modification of design to be as simple as possible, and many other innovative departures all contributed to the speed of construction and the saving of material and dead weight in these ships, which were nicknamed 'Ugly Ducklings'.*

Simple and reliable were the watchwords given by the Admiralty for the design, construction and maintenance of ships for the war. Operation Neptune – the naval component of Operation Overlord, the Allied invasion of Normandy – demonstrated the breadth of shipping required and supplied. A staggering 702 warships, covering battleships, monitors, cruisers, destroyers, sloops, frigates, corvettes, patrol craft and motor launches, took part in the operation.

Left: *Army troops wade ashore at Omaha Beach during the D-Day landings, 6 June 1944. They were brought to the beach by a Coast Guard-manned LCVP (landing craft).*

Below: *View of the Gooseberry breakwater of sunken ships at the east end of the Mulberry 'A' artificial harbour off Omaha Beach, with shipping offshore.*

Mulberry harbours

Mulberry harbours were temporary portable harbours used during World War II to enable the rapid offloading of cargo on to beaches during the Allied invasion of Normandy in June 1944.

Shown here is a Mulberry harbour assembled in preparation for the invasion of Normandy, with military vehicles crossing a floating roadway.

Close to the entrance of Langstone harbour there is a wrecked Phoenix breakwater type C. It was originally constructed to form part of a World War II Mulberry harbour system.

Portland harbour: these are two Phoenix units made of reinforced concrete constructed for use during the follow-up to the Normandy landings.

HMS *Alliance* (P417)

HMS *Alliance* was completed after World War II in 1947. She is a Royal Navy A-class submarine and the only surviving example of her class. She has been a memorial and museum ship since 1981.

Recent claim to fame? In 2017, she was featured in the movie *Transformers: The Last Knight*.

After the war ended, it was obvious that the construction of new vessels would drop off, but global travel was on the up. Surplus and, of course, new aircraft were seen as a fast and easy way to travel the world. By the early 1950s, passenger transport by sea was unable to compete with all the new airlines; by the early 1960s, the number of passengers who flew the Atlantic had grown by 95 per cent. It seemed that the reign of the majestic ocean liners had come to an end ... or had it?!

Seen here are the torpedo hatches. Alliance has six 21 in bow torpedo tubes, four 21 in stern torpedo tubes and can carry 20 torpedoes.

HMY *Britannia*

Generally known as the Royal Yacht *Britannia*, she's the yacht formerly used by the royal family for official engagements. She was launched not long after the war in 1954 and served until 1997. Today she is berthed at Ocean Terminal, Leith, Edinburgh.

Right: *HMY* Britannia *in dock at Leith.*

Below: *A view from above, showing visitors on the Royal Yacht* Britannia, *which is now open to the general public.*

Monsters of the sea

The one area of shipping that thrived post-war was container ships, which could load and unload quickly at docks. Container ships came into their own during the 1950s and became rivals to the huge carriers – oil tankers and bulk carriers – as the largest commercial vessels on the ocean. The scale of these leviathans also affected ports such as London, which was no longer able to deal with these huge commercial vessels.

Main image: *A container ship loaded down with cargo.*

Inset: *Like the vessel shown, the earliest container ships were T2 tankers converted in the 1940s after World War II.*

Daredevil spirit

A phenomenon that caught the public imagination after the war was the record-breaking runs of Donald Campbell in his incredible *Bluebird K7* boat. He began in 1949 and, between 1955 and 1964, Campbell set seven world water speed records. In 1967, he went to Coniston Water, in the Lake District, for another attempt, this time to break the 300 mph barrier. Initially all went well, but calamity struck as *Bluebird* lifted from the lake and somersaulted, before hitting the water and breaking up.

Main image: *Donald Campbell in Bluebird K7 at Coniston Water, Cumbria in 1958, attempting the world water speed record.*

Right: *An exuberant Campbell sitting in K7 in 1959.*

Inset: Bluebird K7 *in dry dock between speed attempts at Lake Mead, USA, 1956.*

Campbell died in the accident, but afterwards Mr Whoppit, his teddy bear mascot, and his helmet were found among the floating debris. Royal Navy divers searched for his body, but after two weeks they called off the search without locating it – his body was eventually found in 2001. He broke eight absolute world speed records on water and on land in the 1950s and 1960s and remains the only person to set both world land and water speed records in the same year (1964).

Memorials and dedications

If you wander around London, and other UK cities, in particular those on the coast, you will often come across memorials and special places dedicated to those who gave their lives, not only in the two world wars but also in the search to advance marine technology and all things related. The memorial at Tower Hill in London is particularly poignant and is dedicated to the men and women of the Merchant Navy and fishing fleets who died in both wars. Others too have their own special local significance.

A view of the front of London's Tower Hill Memorial complex. Walking around it is not just interesting but very moving.

The main image is the Naval Memorial at Plymouth Hoe. It's dedicated to sailors who died in both world wars with no known grave.

Inset top left: *Plaque to Operation Overlord 1944 on the quayside at Poole.*

Inset above: *Memorial to submariners on the Embankment, London.*

Inset left: *My personal favourite is Britannia looking like she really does rule the waves. This too can be found at Plymouth Hoe.*

5 Modern Times

A view from the stern of HMS Ocean, with helicopters clearly visible.

L12

Today's British ships

Following World War II, the steady recession of the British Empire necessitated a decrease in the size of the Royal Navy, with the USA swiftly overtaking the UK as the world's largest navy. In 1945, the Royal Navy still had more than 500 warships, but by 1960 numbers were down to 120. By the time of the Falklands War in 1982, the Royal Navy had half that number, with 60 warships. As a result of substantial cuts to the defence budget in 2010, the last of the light carriers were scrapped.

Not all decommissioned ships are scrapped; many are sold as surplus equipment on a government-to-government basis. In 2018, HMS *Ocean*, helicopter carrier and fleet flagship of the Royal Navy, was sold to Brazil. The money made from selling these ships is then reinvested into defence.

Left: *An Army Air Corps Apache helicopter takes off from HMS* Ocean *during Operation Ellamy, the UK's contribution to United Nations Security Resolution 1973, in the Med off the coast of Libya.*

Below: *US Marines ride the forward aircraft lift into* Ocean's *hangar deck during an exercise in 1999.*

HMS Vanguard *under way at sea, photographed from the island of a British aircraft carrier.*

HMS *Vanguard*

As strategy evolved, some old designs became obsolete. A good example of this is the move away from battleships – huge vessels that served their purpose once but later became vulnerable against aircraft. This prompted a shift towards aircraft carriers as air power became more important.

Many Royal Navy ships, once they become surplus to requirements, are refitted for use in different situations and often sold off to other parties. An example of this was HMS *Vanguard*, which went through several different stages before she was commissioned in 1946, even serving later as a royal yacht for tours worldwide. The initial redesigns echoed lessons that were learned during World War II, which included enhancing fuel capacity and adding extra space between the inboard and outboard propeller shafts. The aim of this was to prevent torpedoes from taking out both propeller shafts if they penetrated the compartment.

The ship's Royal Marine detachment stands to attention on the quarter-deck during the flag-raising ceremony, 12 September 1952. To the rear is the Royal Marine band. Vanguard was about to put to sea with the fleet to begin the NATO exercise, 'Operation Mainbrace'.

Watertight access trunks were also an addition to all spaces below the deep waterline. This was to avert progressive flooding through open watertight doors and hatches, as happened to HMS *Prince of Wales* when she sank. The changes that were made did cause some problems. For example, adding more fuel meant that the ship would sit lower in the water, therefore the 34 ft limit for the Suez Canal was exceeded.

To combat this, the ship was made wider, which then became a problem for docking at Rosyth and Plymouth, and any other narrow dock. The Admiralty decided that *Vanguard* was by now obsolete, too expensive to run and would have to be scrapped. So, on 7 June 1960, she was decommissioned and sold to the Iron and Steel Corporation of Great Britain for £560,000. *Vanguard* was the last battleship to be scrapped.

Heavy seas break over Vanguard's *bow as she makes about 30 knots during a speed run as part of Operation Mainbrace.*

Full power trial

In 1980, HMS *Hermes* was one of the few remaining British carriers. She received a refit to serve as the Carrier Group Flagship and the platform from which Admiral John 'Sandy' Woodward coordinated the naval campaign in the Falklands.

Seen in the foreground is HMS Defender, with INS Viraat (previously HMS Hermes) in the background.

Main image: *HMS* Hermes *seen entering harbour in the Far East.*

Hermes was sold to India in 1986 and renamed INS *Viraat* until July 2018. In 2017, she was decommissioned by the Indian navy and a campaign was started to raise funds to keep her as a museum ship. Sadly, only a fraction of the £100,000 required was offered.

Right: *Harrier GR.3 aircraft of 1 Squadron parked alongside Royal Navy Sea Harriers and a Sea King helicopter on the flight deck of HMS* Hermes *on 19 May 1982, the day that 1 Squadron joined up with* Hermes *in the South Atlantic.*

Falklands War

The Falklands War was the most important operation taken on by the Royal Navy after World War II. In 1982, ships travelled 8,000 miles (12,875 km) to fight a war in the Falkland Islands, off Argentina, and although four naval ships and other Royal Fleet Auxiliary (RFA) ships were lost, the Royal Navy helped to win the conflict. HMS *Conqueror* (seen left) is the only nuclear-powered submarine to have engaged an enemy ship with torpedoes (ARA *General Belgrano*) during the fighting and sunk it.

Inset: *The ARA* Belgrano, *originally the US Navy light cruiser USS* Phoenix *(CL-46), steaming down Battleship Row, Pearl Harbor. In the background are sunken and burning battleships, 7 December 1941.*

179

A famous ship that was lost in the Falklands was the SS *Atlantic Conveyor*, one of a range of British Merchant Navy ships that was requisitioned during the war. These ships were used to carry supplies and aircraft to the islands for the Royal Navy.

On 25 May 1982, the same day as the loss of HMS *Coventry*, *Atlantic Conveyor* was hit by two Exocet missiles fired by Argentine navy Super Étendard jet fighters. The strikes ignited stores of fuel and ammunition and caused an uncontrollable fire. By the time

Main image: *HMS* Coventry *– sunk by Argentine Air Force A-4 Skyhawks on 25 May 1982 during the Falklands War.*

the fire had burnt out, nothing onboard was recoverable. Three out of four Boeing Chinooks and a Westland Lynx were destroyed, meaning that British troops had to march on foot across the Falklands to recapture Stanley, the capital of the islands. The incident involved the deaths of 12 men aboard *Atlantic Conveyor*, including the ship's master, Captain Ian North, who was posthumously awarded the Distinguished Service Cross, and it was the first loss of a merchant vessel at sea to enemy fire since World War II.

Inset: Atlantic Conveyor *approaching the Falkland Islands.*

After World War II, while the British turned their attention to improving the conventional design of the submarine, focus in the United States fell on nuclear-powered vessels, at first submarines and later surface vessels. The application of nuclear energy for marine engines is believed by many to be one of the greatest advances in transport history. The heat caused by the nuclear reaction is used to raise steam into a turbine, which can even be seen as an echo of the industrial past 200 years ago.

While the nuclear option is in many ways more efficient and 'green' than other choices, such as coal or diesel, it comes with its own challenges. These range from the serious – the disposal of nuclear waste in ports and at sea – to the seemingly trivial, the impossibility of ever safely displaying them in museums.

Main image: *Starboard quarter-view of the world's first nuclear-powered attack submarine USS* Nautilus *(SSN 571) moored in a naval shipyard.*

Inset: *Interior of the submarine USS* Nautilus. *Torpedoes are visible on storage racks.*

The seventh HMS *Dreadnought* (seen opposite) was the United Kingdom's first nuclear-powered submarine.

After the first of the US nuclear successes with the USS *Nautilus* in 1955, it took the British Royal Navy another eight years to have its first nuclear-powered submarine. HMS *Dreadnought* was launched in the 1960s, and the introduction of nuclear weapons came with the Resolution class submarines in the form of the Polaris missile.

Left: *The conning tower of HMS* Resolution.

Right: *A Polaris missile launch from* Resolution *in 1983.*

HMS *Astute*

The latest nuclear-powered submarine to be presented to the Royal Navy is the Astute class. These up-to-the-minute submarines are being constructed by BAE Systems Maritime–Submarines at Barrow-in-Furness. In total, seven boats have been ordered, the first of which, *Astute*, was declared fully operational in May 2014.

HMS *Audacious*

Seen here under construction is the fourth Astute-class, nuclear-powered fleet submarine of the Royal Navy. Formally given her name on 16 December 2016, she was launched on 28 April 2017. Her nuclear reactor does not have to be refuelled during the boat's 25-year service as the submarine can purify water and air. Although she is able to circumnavigate the planet without surfacing, supplies of food have to be replenished as she can only carry enough for three months for 98 officers and ratings. As far as weaponry is concerned, she will have provision for up to 38 weapons in six 21-inch torpedo tubes. *Audacious* is capable of using Tomahawk Block IV land-attack missiles with a range of 1,000 miles (1,600 km), and Spearfish heavyweight torpedoes.

RV *Triton*, strangely enough a trimaran, was a research vessel and former prototype British warship demonstrator for the UK's Defence Evaluation and Research Agency (later QinetiQ). She was built as a technology demonstrator ship for the Royal Navy's Future Surface Combatant and has been tested for hull viability and as a trials platform for other innovations. She was used by the Australian Border Forces' Marine Unit (main image), but now rests on the River Yare in Great Yarmouth, Norfolk (right).

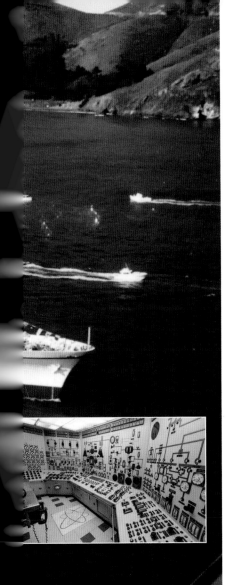

Floating advert

In the 1960s, the NS *Savannah*, the world's first nuclear-powered cargo-passenger ship, was born out of the imagination of US President Dwight Eisenhower. In his 'Atoms for Peace' speech, he attempted to balance the growing fear of nuclear apocalypse with optimism about civilian use of atomic energy. The ship was to be an advert for nuclear energy. In 1964, the *Savannah* set sail on a tour of Europe. Crowds lined docksides and thousands of people, government officials and industrialists among them, boarded to inspect its facilities. However, the civilian nuclear ship never surpassed the diesel-powered design and fell off the commercial shipping industry's radar. The UK pursued its nuclear ambitions mainly in the submarine sector; the first nuclear sub was commissioned into the Royal Navy in 1963.

Main image: *NS* Savannah *passing under the Golden Gate Bridge in 1962.*

Inset: *Her extremely impressive control room.*

At the start of the 1980s, the Royal Navy directed its efforts into anti-submarine warfare (ASM). Its strategy was to search for and, if necessary, destroy Soviet submarines in the North Atlantic and to operate the nuclear deterrent submarine force. The Continuous At Sea Deterrent (CASD) is about the use of Royal Navy submarines armed with Trident nuclear missiles in order to maintain a 365-day-a-year nuclear deterrent for the UK. The purpose of the submarines is to ensure that the deterrent is always present, leaving hostile nuclear states unable to pinpoint the location of missile sites on the mainland in a pre-emptive strike.

A view of HMS Vengeance *returning to Her Majesty's Naval Base (HMNB) Clyde, after completing operational sea training.*

HMS Vengeance *carries the Trident ballistic missile, the UK's nuclear deterrent, as shown here.*

In 2018, we have seen a lot of advances and change in the Royal Navy fleet. The decommissioning and sale of HMS *Ocean* preceded the arrival of the first of the new Queen Elizabeth-class carriers, undergoing tests prior to delivery of her first fixed-wing aircraft. Work is also being carried out on a new generation of nuclear deterrent submarines.

The Royal Navy's new aircraft carrier HMS Queen Elizabeth arrives in Gibraltar for her first overseas port visit. The 65,000-tonne future flagship was conducting a routine logistics stop, having left her home in Portsmouth a week earlier for helicopter trials.

There are plans for two classes of frigate to replace the ageing (but highly effective and rightly feared) T23 class. These will be the Type 26 and the Type 31 frigates.

Main image: *HMS* Dauntless *is the second ship of the Type 45 or 'Daring-class' air-defence destroyers.*

Above: *The Type 26 frigate as proposed by BAE Systems.*

A brief history of containerization

Containerization started quite a while ago, although on a slightly smaller scale, when in the late 18th century James Brindley designed box boats, which were called starvationers because of their exposed ribs. They featured ten open wooden containers in which coal would be transported from Worsley Delph quarry to Manchester via the Bridgewater canal.

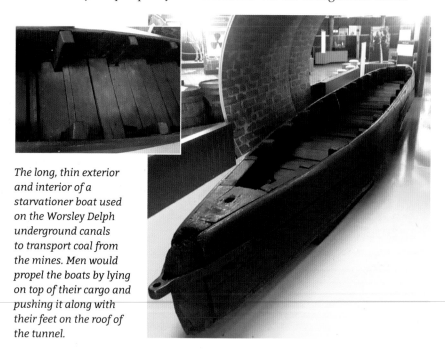

The long, thin exterior and interior of a starvationer boat used on the Worsley Delph underground canals to transport coal from the mines. Men would propel the boats by lying on top of their cargo and pushing it along with their feet on the roof of the tunnel.

Before containerization as we know it was conceived, other types of transportation were used, with canal boats, wagons and railways working together.

Stevedores, as they were known, manually unloading cargo from a ship, c. 1877.

A process began to emerge whereby goods handled manually as break bulk cargo – goods that were transported in bags, boxes, crates, drums or barrels – were loaded on to a vehicle and transported to a port warehouse, where they would be stored awaiting the next vessel. Once the vessel turned up, it would load the goods and make its way to the next stop, possibly to load up more goods or drop some off. This was a slow and costly process and goods would often take long periods of valuable time to arrive at their destination.

By the 1830s, it wasn't only the UK but many other countries around the world where they were using wooden containers that could easily be transferred to other types of transport such as the railroads. These were simple rectangular timber boxes, which for example were used to transport coal from the Lancashire collieries via the Liverpool and Manchester Railway to Liverpool. Here they would be lifted by crane on to horse-drawn carts for their final destination. Wooden boxes were joined by iron ones in the 1840s and, by the early 1900s, closed containers had been adopted.

Mixed cargo being loaded on to ships, c. 1912.

Containerization began to develop and spread after World War II, thus doing away with manual sorting of goods and warehousing costs, along with easing up port congestion, reducing shipping times and losses from damage incurred. On the debit side, due to doing away with break bulk cargo handling, thousands of dock workers lost their jobs.

A busy modern-day container port with all the facilities.

As of 2009, some 90 per cent of non-bulk cargo worldwide has been transported by containers stacked on ships. The statistics of container transport are jaw-dropping. For example, in China alone in 2009, there were 105,976,701 international and coastal (not including Hong Kong) trans-shipments. As ships become even larger and can carry more and more goods, there is talk of size restriction, which will be calculated by the depth

CMA CGM KERGUELEN
LONDON

of the Straits of Malacca – which links the Indian Ocean to the Pacific Ocean – one of the busiest shipping lanes in the world. Forget the Plimsoll line, this will be known as the Malaccamax line. Today, these huge floating monsters transport their cargoes across all the oceans of the world. They are loaded to the gunnels, their containers piled up on deck, as they float majestically on the oceans or even on the deeper rivers of the world.

Kerguelen *is a 17,722 TEU very large UK-flagged Explorer class container ship owned by the French shipping company CMA CGM. As of August 2015, it was the largest container ship in their fleet.*

Cruise ships

Leisure cruising goes back to 1822 with the formation of the Peninsular & Oriental Steam Navigation Company – today's P&O. The company started off as a shipping line and was awarded its first contract to deliver mail in 1837. The first passenger journeys began in 1844, with cruises to such places as Gibraltar, Malta and Athens, all departing from Southampton. P&O Cruises are seen as the world's original cruise line, although according to some sources the ship *Francesco I*, flying the flag of the Kingdom of the Two Sicilies (Italy), is viewed as the first cruise ship ever, although this service was restricted to the nobility and the rich and was never a public commercial enterprise.

RMS Strathaird, *a P&O cruise ship of the early 20th century, with only one funnel after her extensive 1947 refit following wartime service. The company began offering luxury cruise services way back in 1844.*

The success of its cruises saw P&O expand, with new, larger and more luxurious ships being added to the line. Two of the more famous vessels were the SS *Ravenna* from 1880 and the SS *Valetta* built in 1889, the first ship to use electric lights.

The RMS *Campania* built in 1892 and her sister ship RMS *Lucania* were also added for the Cunard Line. There were three luxury liners transporting passengers from Europe to North America in 1897, and this had increased to seven by 1906.

Main image: *The RMS Campania, a British ocean liner of the Cunard Steamship Line, on the River Mersey.*

Inset right is her sister ship the Lucania and below is an advertisement for the Cunard shipping line.

FOR SAFETY COMFORT   TAKE THE OLD RELIABLE

CUNARD LINE

SAILING 4 TIMES A-WEEK   FOR ALL EUROPEAN POINTS

ESTABLISHED 1840

BETWEEN

NEW-YORK LIVERPOOL

CAMPANIA

Queen Elizabeth 2
*moored at Trondheim,
Norway in 2008.*

After World War II, things became tricky for cruise liners as aircraft became far more comfortable; they also delivered their passengers safely and more quickly to their destinations. By the 1960s, with the advent of jet aircraft, the seagoing liner business went into a nosedive. Liners had several serious problems: they were tatty and starting to show their age; they were uneconomical; and they had trouble entering some ports. In 1986, ocean liner services for passengers completely ceased, except for the transatlantic crossings operated by the British Cunard Line. These crossings soon changed from general passenger travel to cruising with entertainment value. This radical shift was pioneered by Cunard and their luxury cruise transatlantic service on the ocean liner *Queen Elizabeth 2*. The crossing was advertised as a holiday in itself and international celebrities were brought in to entertain the guests as part of each evening's cabaret. A whole new chapter had begun in the story of the cruise liner and, with this, newer, larger and more luxurious ships were built to take people on voyages of discovery to exotic parts of the world.

Left: *The* Carnival Fantasy operated by American-British company, the Carnival Cruise Line.

Opposite: Norwegian Gem built by *Meyer Werft*.

Today, the glamorous, new generation of cruise ships are basically floating hotels, with swimming pools, tennis courts and endless entertainment. In the evenings, features are cabaret, bars and restaurants. The passengers are treated like kings and queens and want for nothing on their cruise.

Three major European shipyards now dominate the cruise ship building trade: Italy's Fincantieri, STX France and Germany's Meyer Werft in Papenburg. The biggest cruise ship in the world, *Oasis of the Seas*, is the biggest passenger-carrying ship ever. It's five times the size of the *Titanic*.

MS Queen Elizabeth *moored in Kobe, Japan.*

MS *Queen Elizabeth*, one of the latest additions to the Cunard books, is a beautiful floating palace. Construction took place in Italy between 2007 and 2010 and Her Majesty Queen Elizabeth II officially named the ship at a ceremony that was held at Southampton on 11 October 2010. This was just prior to her maiden voyage to the Canary Islands. She can carry up to 2,092 passengers.

Sailing from Dover in Kent, ferries run around the clock to take people over to the Continent. They travel to different parts of northern Europe. The ships are generally big, comfortable and convenient.

Ferry transportation

We must not neglect the ferries of this world; they carry out a crucial role in the transportation of people as well as trucks and cars. They are part of our everyday public transport systems, to and from many waterside cities and islands. For those of us wanting to take cars abroad, or for those lorry drivers that need to cross the English Channel for example, these ferries are invaluable, quick and generally very accommodating.

Today these ferries carry everything from commercial trucks through to the humble everyday automobile, sometimes with a caravan or trailer. On board, there are cabins for longer overnight trips; they're kitted out with bathrooms and comfortable beds, food and entertainment. Travelling the short distance between Dover and Calais, for example, takes a mere one and a half hours and not only provides a break from driving but gives you the chance to stock up with delicious food, drink and entertainment.

MS Stena Scandinavica *is the first of two identical ships built by Hyundai Heavy Industries, the world's largest shipbuilding company, for Stena Line. There has been an increasing trend for shipping companies to merge with other international companies. In 1998 P&O European Ferries (Dover) Ltd., and the Dover and Newhaven concern of Stena Line merged, creating P&O Stena Line.*

Right: *Although now renamed* Royal Iris, *the* Mountwood *featured in the film* Ferry Cross The Mersey. *She is currently the ferry that crosses the River Mersey every day and, here, she is seen passing the iconic Liver Building in Liverpool.*

P&O ferries Pride of Burgundy *and* Pride of Kent, *seen at the busy port of Dover.*

All kinds of ships now travel the oceans, rivers and waterways of the world, carrying out whatever work they need to do.

Fewer large vessels may now be built in Britain because of costs, but much of the know-how that has led to the amazing technology aboard modern ships is down to Britain and the British.

MS Spirit of Britain *beneath Dover castle.*

Picture credits

Shropshire Historic Environment Record: p12 Top Left; Top Right

VollwertBIT via Wikimedia: p19 Bottom

Eva Kröcher via Wikimedia: p19 Top

US Naval History and Heritage Command Photograph: p20; 86/87; 91; 114/115; 124/125; 128 Inset; 130/131; 132; 134/135; 135; 152/153; 153 Inset; 170/171; 172; 173

theromneymarsh.net: p21

State Library of New South Wales via Wikimedia: p54; 56 Inset

National Library of Australia p53; 56/57

Metropolitan Museum of Art via Wikimedia: p58

American Civil War Museum via Wikimedia: p70

Getty Images: p72/73

National Library of Ireland, Ireland: p74

McLean Museum, Inverclyde Council: p75

State Library of Victoria, Allan C. Green collection of glass negatives via Wikimedia: p76/77; 78/79; 128/129

Alfred Corry Lifeboat Museum: p85

Deutsches Schiffahrtsmuseum Bremerhaven (Allemagne) via Wikimedia: p98

Dave Jenkins - InfoGibraltar via Wikimedia: p98/199

BAE SYSTEMS, UK: p102; 184/185; 201

Bundesarchiv via Wikimedia: p108 Top Right

Crown Copyright – IWM via Wikimedia: p108 Top Left; p118 Bottom; p142/143; 143 Inset

MOD Image: p119; 174/175; 176/177; 176 Inset; 177 Inset; 188/189; 190/191

US Navy Photo: p120; 161; 179

By courtesy of the University of Liverpool Library, Cunard Archive (Stewart Bale) D42-PR2-1-66-C2: p133

Australian War Memorial via Wikimedia: p140/141

Thanks to the Association of Dunkirk Little Ships via Ian Gilbert: p144/145

National Motor Museum, Beaulieu, Hampshire, UK; p162/163

Nicholas Bevan Collection: p164

Photo: L(Phot) Dave Jenkins/MOD: p166/167

Photo: LA(Phot) Guy Pool/MOD: p168/169

CPL Jimmie Perkins, USMC: p169 Inset

www.navyphotos.co.uk: p178/179; 186/187

US Defence Image: p180/181; 187 Inset

DM Gerard via Wikimedia: p181 Inset

kenhodge13 via Wikimedia: p192/193

Photo: POA(Phot) Tam McDonald/MOD: p196

Lockheed Martin: p197

US Navy photo by Lt. Cmdr. Corey Barker: p200/201

Kees Torn via Wikimedia: p206/207

Trondheim Havn via Wikimedia: p212/213

Spaceaero2 via Wikimedia: p216/217

Stena Line via Wikimedia: p220/221

Michiel Hendryckx via Wikimedia P222/223

US National Archives, Washington DC USA

US Library of Congress, Washington DC USA

Other images from the Mirco De Cet Archive (mircodecet.com)